DISRUPTIVE LITERACY

DR DHEERAJ MEHROTRA

Copyright © Dr Dheeraj Mehrotra
All Rights Reserved.

This book has been published with all efforts taken to make the material error-free after the consent of the author. However, the author and the publisher do not assume and hereby disclaim any liability to any party for any loss, damage, or disruption caused by errors or omissions, whether such errors or omissions result from negligence, accident, or any other cause.

While every effort has been made to avoid any mistake or omission, this publication is being sold on the condition and understanding that neither the author nor the publishers or printers would be liable in any manner to any person by reason of any mistake or omission in this publication or for any action taken or omitted to be taken or advice rendered or accepted on the basis of this work. For any defect in printing or binding the publishers will be liable only to replace the defective copy by another copy of this work then available.

Contents

Preface

Disruptive Literacy is a priority. We observed the Learning losses during this pandemic have unfortunately been high, potentially limiting students in the future. Here comes the paging of the new normal within the classrooms of today. The pandemic delay and the miss have had their reach in very different formats. It encapsulated the structure to regulate the priorities in view.

The book Disruptive Literacy enhances the notion and readily activates the learning in the new format with the uncertain world.

Author

www.authordheerajmehrotra.com

ONE

DISRUPTIVE LITERACY: WHAT & WHY?

<hr>

Friends, Disruptive Literacy defines the new phase of learning against all odds.

Though the pandemic was a hard time for all, the ones affected and set on a path to an unsteady, unclear future, where the world's marginalised children. The pandemic has been a long and hard road with a distant end.

Quote Unquote:

"In March, we will mark two years of COVID-19-related disruptions to global education. We are looking at a nearly unimaginable loss to children's schooling," said Robert Jenkins, UNICEF Chief of Education. "While the disruptions to learning must end, just reopening schools is not enough. Students need intensive support to recover lost education. Schools must also go beyond places of learning to rebuild children's mental and physical health, social development and nutrition."

It has caused worldwide distress and a new type of disadvantage for children. No longer is the summer slide the area to fear; it is the literacy slide that went on despite teachers' efforts to make remote schools similar to prepandemic schools. Hence we, educators, roll out disruptive literacy and monitor the learning that lacks today's classrooms in particular.

Out of nowhere, I went over this word VUCA, Volatile, Uncertain, Complex, and Ambiguous, distinguishing the new world request of range with no decision except for an approach to confronting the difficulties changing over them into favourable circumstances.

Without a doubt, the world is confronting a difficult time today. Nobody was at any point arranged for this and will at any moment be. The need we the people must have a deduction *today towards having a bunch of essential abilities, information and demeanour, and business purchases these at a cost.*

Understanding the VUCA World, the better! The abbreviation VUCA - Volatile, Uncertain, Complex, and Ambiguous - was authored during the 1990s. It depicts numerous individuals' experiences of their work environment

incredibly well.

In this climate, it tends to be challenging to feel like you are adapting - not to mention flourishing. The abbreviation VUCA - Volatile, Uncertain, Complex, and Ambiguous - was instituted during the 1990s. It depicts numerous individuals' experiences of their work environment amazingly well. In the learning environment, the learners, particularly the students, need to return to a supportive, friendly atmosphere, where their learning loss and socio-emotional needs are recognised, dwelled, and curated as per the new world order and acknowledged by the educators at large. These notions and craftings are required to help them get back on track. One of the key lessons learnt throughout the crisis is the importance of engaging parents and communities in pupils' learning process. And this must continue!

In this climate, it may be not easy to feel like you are adapting - not to mention flourishing. Driving in a VUCA World - Leadership in the hours of Crisis is the new world order. We truly are seeing a remarkable change on the planet, and no part of our life is immaculate by this

change.

From the unexpected change in our way of life to the tremendous shift in mentality, the present circumstance has constrained us to think fast, extraordinary, and raise versatility. Professional life is the same. In the genuine sense, the world right currently exemplifies the VUCA reasoning; Volatile, Uncertain, Complex, and Ambiguous. We were not ready for this unexpected development, and many are confused about how to adapt to this and push forward. Convenient solutions will presently don't work; this change is somewhat perpetual.

It implies that we should rethink and re-adjust every technique for activity, thinking, acting, and being. Going ahead, mental and enthusiastic well-being balance has gotten basic on an ongoing premise. The capacity to re-adjust ranges of abilities, practices, and activities according to the progressions on the planet is a consuming worry for us all. We are affected by this in some structure or the other. What is required is Mental Health, Resilience, Self consideration and inclusivity. On the off chance that organisations and organisations are unequipped for sympathy, we can venture up and connect with companions and family members in trouble. The Covid times require that extra portion of local area administration and social awareness for sure companions. We can start a little—every single one of us. Keeping yourself propelled in any event, during the current situation where there is torment ..enduring ..passing .. lockdown.. dejection.. the world has halted. Inspiration comes from the inside.. equilibrium of the brain-body soul. In this infuriating situation, keep a quiet, adjusted, formed outlook .. keeping yourself propelled, self-inspired, and forcing others as the new practice.

"Keeping yourself roused in any event, during the current situation". Much as we like to consider these as reasonable and impartial and fearlessly take cutbacks in our step, the playing. At the point when an acquiring part loses his employment, the family's funds are seriously affected.

This is undoubtedly Sad and lamentable. The vulnerability is troubling. A few families think it's extreme to try and meet routine costs—some need to plunge into their resources. The family and the business are extraordinary in strength and holding power. Like this, they need to see conservations and cutbacks with the unfortunate moments.

In this way, the individuals who have lost their positions are taking a gander at a significant stretch of joblessness, cooped up for the most

part inside their homes. Many would have managed their circumstance in protection without upsetting the family. What would we be able to do is comes a priority for all at this hour as educators too on importance. Start Small, Start some online business. Investigate some revenue of yours as a calling. Check the old recollections to be content. Have a go at cutting your costs and requests. Be together. Efficient attempt alternatives. They search for various acquiring choices regardless of whether they are more minor or excellent. Beware of conveying on the web range of instructing/preparing/directing/the majority worldwide.

That is absolutely how I felt! As an educator. The teaching is on with no real students, in real-time physical classrooms. The learning is on but for sure at the independence of the learner. Likewise, preparation members and workshop crowds have been getting some information for quite a long time. So I chose to gather the ten best apparatuses and standards I know into a short, sharp course. Quite possibly, the most significant way to deal with flourishing in a VUCA world is the Pareto Principle, the 80:20 standard. The 80:20 principle says that you get 80% of the worth from the best 20% of the thoughts, and we end up applying it when you use it skillfully. In this way, here is the best 20%. Apply it well, and you'll immensely affect your prosperity at work. Learning how to learn is the new priority.

The Uncertain Times!

"There are two things we can say with conviction about the future: it will be extraordinary. Like never before, pioneers need to explore new testing times, a reviving speed of progress, expanding assumptions, and a rising tide of quickly developing conditions. This unique and distinctive climate (VUCA) is moving pioneers to discover better approaches to lead their associations and make supported progress. Because of these conditions, there is a hunger for administration. Yet, pioneers face a tornado climate loaded with incredible freedoms and overwhelming difficulties in leading their kin and associations.

If I share the quote by Prof Sattar Bawany (2019), the Fourth Industrial Revolution (Industry 4.0) addresses a blend of Artificial Intelligence, Robotics, Cyber-Physical Systems and the Internet-of-Things (IoT). Authority 4.0 is about pioneers making their advanced change procedure and guaranteeing that it is lined up with their business's business and development plans. This is accomplished by successfully showing the set-up of next-generation initiative capabilities, which incorporate basic reasoning and imaginative speculation alongside enthusiastic and social knowledge abilities like sympathy and relationship with the board.

Driving in the Fourth Industrial Revolution (Industry 4.0) spins around overseeing difficulties in a business climate that is profoundly problematic, progressively computerised and overwhelmingly unstable, unsure, mind-boggling and vague (VUCA). Innovative headways in artificial brainpower, mechanical technology, sharing stages and the Internet of Things adjust action plans and businesses. These progressions are occurring at an uncommon speed. Pioneers at all levels must foster the significant capabilities and abilities to effectively adapt to new fundamental factors when driving in a troublesome VUCA World.

VUCA is an abbreviation that arose out of the military during the 1990s. It portrays the "haze of war" — the turbulent conditions experienced in an advanced combat zone. Its importance to pioneers in business is evident, as these conditions elucidate the climate where the company is led each day. Authority, not surprisingly, including making a dream, isn't sufficient in a VUCA world. TEACHING IN THE VUCA WORLD, a card priority fetches the world of uncertainties. The new world order of VOLATILE, UNCERTAIN, COMPLEX, and AMBIGUOUS approaches reflects a new everyday learning and exploring the novel working order.

• Volatile: Things change eccentrically, out of nowhere, very, particularly for the more regrettable.

• Uncertain: Important data isn't known or clear; suspicious, hazy about the current circumstance and future results; not ready to be depended upon.

• Complex: Many unique and associated parts: key choice factors, the connection between assorted specialists, development, variation, coevolution, feeble signs.

• *Ambiguous: Open to more than one translation; the significance of an occasion can be perceived unexpectedly.*

Driving in a VUCA world not just gives a moving climate to pioneers to work and for chief advancement program to have an effect: it likewise gives an essential scope of new abilities. The new truth is acknowledging that new and various skills are required for pioneers to prevail in this new typical.

As educators, we need to guide our students and parents towards new destinations, which may include:

Flourish amid unpredictability, vulnerability, intricacy and equivocalness.

Recognise the need to choose what you centre around

Construct an essential organisation of essential contacts

Realise were to work at your pinnacle

Output your frame of reference for changes, patterns, dangers and openings

Bridle the basic achievement framework for life during the transition; the Powerhouse Loop

The Online Teaching and Learning with the Parents Support

Finally, to explore the wonders amongst the PANDEMIC and the readiness to the VUCA world, without a doubt, the word VUCA causes some cocked eyebrows. It characterises the prepared idea of shock, an evoke stun, shock, or offence, ordinarily through whimsical activities or talks. The expression regularly recommends negative consideration or judgment. However, my dear companions serve a reality today.

As a head of a school, I discover checking and testing quickly of solace for the educators to be locked in and module to the learning situation. The range deceives our arrangement which screens. Thus, training has changed drastically with the unmistakable ascent of e-learning, whereby education is attempted distantly and in advanced stages. The paging is organised and characterised by the characteristic of conveying the classes without any difficulty and solace to their takers.

The target of this module enacts learning concerning the Leading Change in a Pandemic

VUCA World specifically. The shared vision and the methodology characterise the destinations with the introduction of understanding the idea in Visualizing the learning incredibly. It incorporates the model to deal with the world through VOCA in the COVID period. Step-by-step instructions to prepare pioneers to oversee through. The idea represents Volatility, Uncertainty, Complexity, and Ambiguity, as VOCA practically speaking.

Without a doubt, as training suppliers, our great work is to help everybody by giving quality schooling, even on these extraordinary occasions. In reality, educators will generally do twofold and surprisingly threefold the task to convey. As we scramble to adapt to the quickly evolving COVID-19 circumstance, many of us are unexpectedly taking on jobs as all-day guardians and substitute educators, along with

the walk for the rush to convey.

The live streaming that the guardians requested some time in the distant past mirror the ascent of new requests and wants. It is required to convey the exercises to give every understudy customised criticism and work on, setting them up to benefit from study hall guidance.

Happy Learning to all on priority.

Ref:

https://www.asmaindia.in/slc-2021/speaker/dr-dheeraj-mehrotra/

TWO

EDUDEMIC OR PANDEMIC?

Post-COVID- An End to Online Befooling!The Edudemic.

For sure, the alarming spectrum delivers the learning to the aspect of teaching online for schools has been in action over a couple of years. For sure, the third wave proved the disinterest attributes in action. The schools are sorry to involve the students and the parents with promises to keep but not in motion. The online spectrum is a failed projection and has been proved majorly. Alarming. We call the call. No education. No Schooling? But a fancy TECH Candy integration. Sorry to say!

Well, the priority is low to spectrum. The teachers find the classrooms empty. The children are away from connecting. The learning is diminishing to zero! What are we up to? Surprisingly the defined approach towards learning is taken a back seat to the segment which relates to once a priority. The activation desires the ready reckoner to manage education by the concerned, including the Government. In India, we aim to approach comfort and safety with the closure of schools. On that note, the segment manages the outcome towards many other elections-related excuses. For sure, the scientific evidence for schools as COVID-19 hotspots is fragile. A study in Spain looked at data from over 1 million children of all ages in schools and found that the R-Value (Rate of Virus Spread) is well less than one for all school students. The R-value is lower for lower ages and as low as 0.2 for pre-primary children; hence, the practice of closing schools appears unscientific.

How do I, as an educator, manage that? Can online learning be the ultimate solution to tasks? Not so, surprisingly so. Teachers and the parents need to gel together to prioritise learning with the conjunction towards learning as a prime approach rather than grasp the notion of closure of schools with the spectrum towards safety. Bells are ringing in countries where we have a heavy load of cases. But for sure, taking a measure like this is like closing the chapters of learning for the future workforce for some time. This may lead to a bleak future for the nation in particular. I stand firm to undertaking as a priority.

My personal experience as a head of school highlights a novel spectrum to route this significance for the cause of quality education. The ratio is bleak towards the unaware specified interest of the students via the online or offline learning segment. The educators need a preface to the exact detail and relate at large numbers via brainstorming to narrate the strategies to follow up in directive for a better cause. The system needs to be re-framed on how best to deliver the knowledge of the new age and the attention to live with corona as a striker for the new page for living and learning.

The concern remains unanswered. Is it a pandemic scarier or the Edudemic? The bridge constructed between online and remote learning has to take a page with the march of time. We just cannot and better never forget the standard portals for the classrooms and their importance. This bridge of learning gap that COVID has widened has also resulted in the investment in the infrastructure to a large extent. The purpose also dwells on the move on the additional emphasis on well-being and reskilling being promoted by the boards specifically. No doubt in terms of boosting the long-term growth but also counts on the importance of re-opening the schools on priority.

Quoting one of the write-ups' by Janmejaya Sinha, Chairman, BCG India, "With due respect to school education, the situation is dire. Data shows that more than 70% of the students have not received significant educational input online. A one-time package for the safe reopening of schools is required. The majority of India's one million schools have closed for two years. Some have been used as vaccination/ isolation centres. As we look to open in 2022, physical infrastructure needs to be revamped, and provisions for forward-looking health and safety measures.

We as educators reflect a measure on the devastating impact of school closure, as by closing schools for this extended and providing just online education; we have violated children's rights in a big way unconsciously. Even the unreasonable response to Omicron has impacted children significantly. Unfortunately, the schools have become an easy and soft target for politicians; closing the schools provides them with the benefit of being seen as "doing something" to being "Caring and Concerned" to containing COVID 19.

The concern lies in measuring whether it may be for the reality of online learning, with no experiential learning, with no interaction in a real sense; the question remains unanswered: Does online education constitute education? I wonder and worry both. It is for sure a poor replacement for physical classes. The children, mainly in the pre-primary and the primary, can learn and be socially and emotionally involved. Quoting the survey report, from Sept. 2021, students' reading and writing levels have declined, with nearly half of them unable to read more than a few rods. More than a third of them were not studying at all.

We, the educator, reflect on the learning with a preface of Priority Learning first among ourselves as the students use their home classrooms, substituting their living rooms as learning platforms professionally. This has come by storm to page their comfort and capsuled their intelligence to a limit only with no physical connection and disruptions like that of actual classrooms. This makes their yesterdays as today and tomorrow with a stereotype living spectrum, targeting their limited learning and limited knowledge as a preface.

The answer lies in our heads, not the search via the laptops.

THREE

WOW CLASSROOMS- A REQUISITE!

WOW Classrooms: A requisite Through Street Smart Teachers!

Marching learning trends have had their toll with the manipulation of Teachers' Choice and their knowledge expertise. Education has taken its pace to the majority who, by chance or tribes, get governed by the Google Generation of today. Alas, to the say, the teachers are no longer the fountain of knowledge but artistic adults to handle the discipline in the classrooms. WOW-Wonder of Wonders must be a reality rather than a should approach within classrooms.

The teachers who motivate, differentiate, make content relevant and leave no student behind are more important than any other factor. Students like the subject only when they like the teacher, hence a directly proportional element within a classroom. The drive by the teacher in the class with the vocabulary is signified by the equilibrium of learning together rather than teaching. They say, "Teachers know the best", activates wisdom in the say but action. The sole reason for this far-fetched approach lies in the nutshell element of a straightforward process of open knowledge, which is unrestricted, versatile and dual with surprises. The satisfaction and the wow part within classrooms only prevails where there is a taste of "It is in the book, Ma'am, tell us something new!" As a teacher, it is our wisdom to teach the "I can do approach" instead of the "I shall try approach, " which is universally possible only when we use kind words in the class. Compliment each kid, especially the difficult ones. That might be the only positive thing they hear all day.

Activating a student-oriented rather than a task-oriented classroom requires more of a relationship with the student. At times apologising to students is a learning moment. If we want kids with character, we must model it to them with others, as character counts. The experiences shared in totality that a genuine apology requires freely admitting fault, fully accepting responsibility, a humbled asking for forgiveness, immediately changing the behaviour and actively rebuilding the trust. The dose of willingness to explore knowledge is what is desired rather than sharing contents from the book. When students appear crusaders of expertise, the teachers must act more like facilitators but strict disciplinarians. It must be apparent to one and all that there is no expiry date for hunger for learning. Let yearning for knowledge be a priority rather than an occasional occurrence. Also, the teachers must explore the power of curing ignorance as the chief element of choice in every interaction with the students, teachers, peers and parents. It is never too late to improve yourself; it should be the priority. The reality segment lies in engaging the children in the class with no fear but intimacy and a feeling of pride both by the students and the teachers. To the real concerns, the fear kills dreams more than failure ever will, which should be mounted on priority by the masses. The children should be made to enjoy the classroom session with engagement and knowledge sharing using ICT tools and techniques of the cyber world and making their Online reputation management a reality.

The students today are no longer kids but young adults and hence need recognition as individuals and partners in the learning process. Critical thinking must be one of the prime qualities of the children as it is among the first causes for change, but is a parish in schools- for no other reason than it conditions the mind to suspect the form and function of everything it sees, including the classroom scenario, all what is taught and discussed. As a teacher, it is our prime requisites to make progress visible, adjust grading practices, model desired habits and not get carried away with the politics of the school, the students and the parents. Hey, the voice violates, the Principal's lobby is rushed for, is there any debating subject rises or fumes up. The school principal is targeted and reassured support to the students, as ever be.

To govern and sense student's friendly classroom, the teachers need to check on their share of the day, of some new vocabulary and make a haze to the fact that the students should be held accountable for the number and the quality of questions students ask and pursue during the teaching-learning process. Right from Good Morning Wishing to the, Thank you, children, the time and share has to be so friendly and empowering to make them take home moments of joy and some attributes to share with their parents. This must be a priority. Teachers must show in action that they are not perfect and never will be. They must take risks with their teaching, and failing must be a part of the learning process. For we are facing the Google Generation, which empowers self and is not dependent on the library or the teacher, fortunately, or unfortunately, I doubt my words too.

The wonderful words help our children use many beautiful words in their writings. We must not blame them for their handwriting and knowledge limitations. Instead, they must be part and parcel of their learning. Also, to create a rapport with the students, the teaching tools in practice by the teachers must be evaluated concerning whether the usage during the lesson is appropriate. With this, the teacher's subject knowledge, enthusiasm, methods of questioning, exposition, and problem-solving related to the multilevel dimension for judging. The teachers as facilitators explore and expose the learning objectives in a big bang way via repartees and the responses generated after every class or via the Parents' Teachers' Meetings on jolt and achievements. Let us conclude the fact that children will love and explore their presence in the classrooms only when given the recognition of individual concerns; teachers must call the kids by their first names keeping them at pace to importance rather than experiencing the only preface with them at the time of the roll calls and that too with referencing through roll numbers.

The choice is ours, engage or enrage! Let quality be the taste forever instead of being just an occasional occurrence. The priority must be to create a WOW classroom with the tongue of "You can do wonders", "You can do it!" and above all ", All my students are the best of the students, and I am proud of them".

FOUR

THE ROYAL TEACHING WITHIN CLASSROOMS

The Royal Shift in Teaching Within Classrooms- From Vedas to You-tubes!

The Indian Education System, due to the widespread illiteracy, has its history now. To the surprise of many, the country has successfully adapted its quality education framework to global standards since its Independence. The learning within schools since the Independence has had its say of reputation and choice by the millions of reach. Thanks to the private players who hand in hand projected literacy with the modulated mechanism set via National Education Framework over the years from time to time. Over the years, we have travelled far from blackboards to digital boards and from Namastay to Hello to Google Framework.

Much of the best reliable approaches for training analysis have headed out of design recently. Many children fail the fractures due to entire language reviewing programs. Unlike phonics-based analysis, natural language does not provide impaired children with the devices to discover brand-new words. These youngsters, since they do not have an all-natural impulse for checking out that is also created as various other youngsters-- merely never learn to review from entire language alone. Unlike yesterday, schools today have a changed adoption of QUALITY as a choice for all the stakeholders, particularly the Teachers, Students and Parents at large.

Still, in some cases, exploratory education and learning function much better than a traditional, educator-driven class version. When pupils are tested to ask about concerns and address troubles, they learn how to assume by themselves. While they're doing this, naturally, they reach establish mathematical, analysis, and scientific research abilities. It does not help all youngsters; however, it is an excellent program for many. Some trainees require an extra organised class, so separating your time between various reliable training techniques is essential. This way, the pupils that such as to pay attention to talks and those that such as to discover by themselves obtain something. With the increase in the education budget every year, India has been progressing with a wave of QUALITY education of International repute of sense and longevity to its totality.

Being a great instructor indicates finding out reliable training techniques. Numerous instructors like to pick one approach and also persevere at all times. Some individuals design themselves as disciplinarians, counting on an old-fashioned enlightening system that calls for outright obedience. Other individuals take a very easygoing strategy, providing their pupils as much flexibility as feasible and thinking that knowledge needs to originate from within. The most effective instructors, nonetheless, are the versatile ones. They do not have their very own animal-efficient mentor approaches. Instead, they agree to take techniques from anywhere that functions.

Many the moments, individuals fail on a reliable training approach. Issues that seem mainly behaviour commonly happen as an outcome of discovering impairments. Youngsters that have problem analysis may begin to act out of stress. The college areas, at the same time, often will undoubtedly capture them acting out without managing the resource of it-- the reality that the youngster cannot check out.

The good news is that there are many reliable mentor techniques to assist in finding out disabled children. Utilising word checklists, phonics policies, mnemonic tools, as well as several various other academic practices, these youngsters can find out to check out. Remarkably sufficient. Nevertheless, these are several of the most efficient training approaches for other trainees. There are locations where the old methods are the very best. The priority and recognition of special education, health education, and technology in education have all framed mechanisms in making our country's educational strata a benchmark for the nations.

Long way to go, we, the educators, have a unique and noble spectrum, but what is required the most is a special status for the teachers, as nation builders, unlike other professions available today. The work needs special attention and priority over others with much of benefits and respect for choices today.

Cheers & Happy Teaching!

FIVE

INTEGRATING NLP WHILE TEACHING!

❦

We are integrating NLP in delivering Education Excellence!

NLP- Integrates unleashing the power for success and happiness. Academics is just another kingdom to deliver the essence!

Neuro-Linguistic Programming, NLP derives the essence of learning via

Neuro: Which integrates the five senses, Visual, auditory, kinesthetic, olfactory and Gustatory. Visual includes Sights:: Auditory defines sounds we hear:: Kinesthetic defines external feelings like a touch of someone or something:: Olfactory means smell:: Gustatory means taste!

Linguistic: Defines the language and other nonverbal communication systems through which our neural representations are coded and include pictures, sounds, feelings, tastes, smells and words.

Programming is the art of discovering and utilising the instructions we run as our communication to ourselves and others to achieve our specific and desired outcomes. It is a tested and progressive model of communicating with ourselves and others. It was initially developed by Richard Bandler, John Grinder and others.

The productivity of individuals is explored to the best via the incentives generated by experience and target vision in particular.

In academics, as a novice spectrum, the NLP integrates into discovering the art of knowing the students with their level of acceptance and learning in totality. It is like using the language of the mind to consistently achieve our specific and desired outcomes to deliver the knowledge aimed at the students. Based on the teachers' experience in the classrooms, the exploring is delivered via the following:

a.

    We are establishing rapport with individual students, enabling you to help them better and create a win-win situation for everyone.

b.

    Have a rapport with the group of students by using pacing and leading. Use this to redirect the entire group to your schedule while remaining in charge.

c.

    Teaching students using the primary senses entrails determining the student's immediate sense system and then delivering information in a way that works best for that system.

d.

They are learning how to read students' minds by learning how to read their eye movements.

e.

Exploring and identifying the balance between suitable brain days and left brain days. Determining which mode the class is in and then teaching in a manner appropriate to the mood of the day.

The subjective analysis within the classrooms attracts practical communication skills from teachers and replicates them to the students. The concept integrates the language of the mind to achieve our specific and desired outcomes consistently. The education delivery with excellence after identifying the audience's traits is art being explored via this. This is indeed a great way to facilitate change. It allows us to be in a position without concern or problem. The mindset is a policy here to deliver the best. Some of the ratios which govern this aspect of curing intelligence by educators involve a push, getting out of the comfort zone, shy zone, arranging a massive paradigm shift, discussing the passion, learning to learn from the environment, must feel most alive, need to be happy in your skin, give oneself a round of applause, empower the limiting belief and the negative emotions about self. Classroom teaching is a nourishing talent which crops with the march of time and tide. Behavioural flexibility narrates the positive outcome only through the sensory acuity and psychology of excellence.

The teaching techniques need to excel with the 'wow' feature with a positive belief by the educators. The nurturing keys to an achievable outcome follow as follows:

- *Being positive*

- *Specified present situation*

- *Specified outcome*

- *Specified evidence procedure*

- *Self-initiated and self-maintained*

- *Appropriately contextualised*

- *Must be ecological*

The approaches govern a practical approach to "All I need is within me now !" let the teachers approach students with a say, "Raise your hand high and tall and say YES !" to promote a sense of agility and promptness during the sessions. The excellence we point to activates with the six human needs of our students and the educators; in particular, the activation delivers via Certainty, Uncertainty/ Variety, Love & Connection, Significance, Growth and Contribution. All of these replicate confidence and provide the power to perform. As teachers, we need to abide by the presuppositions of the NLP, which act like convenient assumptions. It is a requisite desire to respect the other person's world model; the behaviour and change are to be evaluated in context and Ecology. The resistance in a client (student) is a real sign of a lack of rapport. People (pupils) are not their behaviours; everyone is doing the best one can with the available resources, and every behaviour is motivated by positive intent. As a teacher, one must calibrate behaviour as the essential information about a person's behaviour.

Mirroring in classrooms: As teachers, the Mirroring technique of NLP distinguishes the matching portions of another person's behaviour, as in a mirror. This justifies the learning and the learner and the interest between them.

Modelling with children: This is another crucial technique to set the process of learning where we elicit the strategies, filter patterns and physiology that allows someone to produce a specific behaviour. This can be further tackled, modelled and paced as required.

Pacing with Children: This activates the conclusion. It delivers the matching or mirroring of another person's external behaviour to gain rapport. The joy with the kids encounters ease and perforates learning as a result.

The spectrum of learning for fun gets via this NLP, which suffices to the limitations of dissatisfaction among the masses, particularly the stakeholders viz. the students and the parents. Activation of this would undoubtedly result in penetration to learning as a habit rather than an occasional occurrence.

References:

www.nlpforeducators.com

https://yourstory.com/2017/02/a5ef2268e9-nlp-in-academics/

https://www.youtube.com/watch?v=wCphVA3dtEg

https://schools.entrancezone.com/nlp-in-academics-an-initiative-towards-excellence-dheeraj-mehrotra/

http://www.lulu.com/shop/dheeraj-mehrotra/integrating-nlp-towards-excellence-in-academics/paperback/product-23118984.html

http://slideplayer.com/slide/8957695/

SIX

LEARNING EXCELLENCE: A REQUISITE!

To learn is to be aware of the requisites of life and Quality Awareness to the mount of "FIFA World Cup Finalists" to the historical meeting of KIM & TRUMP in Singapore, all nurturing fascination among our learners.

Marching learning trends have had their toll on manipulating Teachers' choices and their knowledge and expertise. Education has taken its pace to the majority who, by chance or tribes, get governed by the Google Generation of today. Alas, to the say, the teachers are no longer the fountain of knowledge but artistic adults to handle the discipline in the classrooms. WOW-Wonder of Wonders must be a reality rather than a should approach within classrooms.

The teachers who motivate, differentiate, make content relevant and leave no student behind are more important than any other factor. Students like the subject only when they like the teacher, hence a directly proportional element within a classroom. The drive by the teacher in the class with the vocabulary is signified by the equilibrium of learning together rather than teaching. They say, "Teachers know the best", activates wisdom in the say but action. The sole reason for this far-fetched approach lies in the nutshell element of a straightforward process of open knowledge, which is unrestricted, versatile and dual with surprises. The satisfaction and the wow part within classrooms only prevail where there is a taste of "It is in the book, Ma'am, tell us something new!" As a teacher, it is our wisdom to teach the "I can do approach" instead of the "I shall try approach, " which is universally possible only when we use kind words in the class. Compliment each kid, especially the difficult ones. That might be the only positive thing they hear all day.

Activating a student-oriented rather than a task-oriented classroom requires more of a relationship with the student. At times apologising to students is a learning moment. If we want kids with character, we must model it to them with others, as character counts. The experiences shared in totality that a genuine apology requires freely admitting fault, fully accepting responsibility, a humbled asking for forgiveness, immediately changing the behaviour and actively rebuilding the trust. The dose of willingness to explore knowledge is what is desired rather than sharing contents from the book. When students appear crusaders of expertise, the teachers need to act more like facilitators but strict disciplinarians. It must be apparent to one and all that there is no expiry date for hunger for learning. Let yearning for knowledge be a priority rather than an occasional occurrence. Also, the teachers must explore the power of curing ignorance as the chief element of choice in every interaction with the students, teachers, peers and parents. It is never too late to improve yourself; it should be the priority. The reality segment lies in engaging the children in the class with no fear but intimacy and a feeling of pride both by the students and the teachers. To the real concerns, fear kills dreams more than failure ever will, which should be mounted on priority by the masses. The children should be made to enjoy the classroom session with engagement and knowledge sharing using ICT tools and techniques of the cyber world and making their Online reputation management a reality.

The students today are no longer kids but young adults and hence need recognition as individuals and partners in the learning process. Critical thinking must be one of the prime qualities of the children as it is among the first causes for change, but is a parish in schools-for no other reason than it conditions the mind to suspect the form and function of everything it sees, including the classroom scenario, all what is taught and discussed. As a teacher, it is our prime requisites to make progress visible, adjust grading practices, model desired habits and not get carried away with the politics of the school, the students and the parents. Hey, the voice violates, the Principal's lobby is rushed for, is there any debating subject rises or fumes up. The school principal is targeted and reassured support to the students, as ever be. The teachers need to adopt Teaching Strategies to consider a WOW factor at all intervals as a habit to enhance learning.

To govern and sense student's friendly classroom, the teachers need to check on their share of the day, of some new vocabulary and make a haze to the fact that the students should be held accountable for the number and the quality of questions students ask and pursue during the teaching-learning process. Right from Good Morning Wishing to the, Thank you, children, for the time and share has to be so friendly and empowering to make them take home moments of joy and some attributes to share with their parents. This must be a priority. Teachers must show in action that they are not perfect and never will be. They must take risks with their teaching, and failing must be a part of the learning process. For we are facing the Google Generation, which empowers self and is not dependent on the library or the teacher, fortunately, or unfortunately, I doubt my words too.

The beautiful words help our children use a wide range of wonderful words in their writings. We must not blame them for their handwriting and knowledge limitations. Instead, they must be part and parcel of their learning. Also, to create a rapport with the students, the teaching tools in practice by the teachers must be evaluated concerning whether the usage during the lesson is appropriate. With this, the teacher's subject knowledge, enthusiasm, methods of questioning, exposition, and problem-solving related to the multilevel dimension for judging. The teachers as facilitators explore and expose the learning objectives in a big bang way via repartees and the responses generated after every class or via the Parents' Teachers' Meetings on jolt and achievements. Let us conclude the fact that children will love and explore their presence in the classrooms only when given the recognition of individual concerns; teachers must call the kids by their first names keeping them at pace to importance rather than experiencing the only preface with them at the time of the roll calls and that too with referencing through roll numbers. The spectrum towards learning to learn as a hobby for both the teachers and the students must stand apt and firm as a lifelong activity.

The choice is ours, engage or enrage! Let quality be the taste forever instead of just an occasional occurrence. The priority must be to create a WOW classroom with the tongue of "You can do wonders", "You can do it!" and above all ", All my students are the best of the students, and I am proud of them". The teachers ought to encapsulate learning as a new pace of Teaching Pattern towards for students look out on demand the novel phase of "It is already in the book, Teach us new!" segment and hence it is a requisite towards Learning first then Teaching as a mechanism by all of us on priority!

SEVEN

PREPARING EDUCATORS

Teachers, Educators or Knowledge Seekers all view depending on technology for the essence of knowledge.

The need for today's teaching segment has dwelled on intelligence and IT-friendly requisites. Quality Education is reflected by the involvement of the Quality Infrastructure in the learning arena, which otherwise is not of any use and Children Friendly. The parents are requested to make their choices today for admission in the majority of the mushrooming shops around the country, more like any other service industry with the option to have a round around the School, the classes and even they *are told to leave their wards in the class as a trial run for them to decide of taste. Computers, software, CDs and Smart Toys ought to be considered as a supplement to the other, more concrete learning activities like completing puzzles, building with Lego and blocks, reading books, creating art projects and playing on the playground...", is evident by our observations and research, out of the present day scenario. On very grounds of improvement planning and the paradigm shift with education characterised by technology-enabled instructions, collaborative learning, multidisciplinary problem-solving and critical thinking skills, **e-learning**, a household name for students today, offers a wide variety of ICT-enabled classroom solutions for learning the Smart Way! It allows a user-friendly option for the learner to integrate what is desired and acquired to their requirements class and level-wise.*

No wonder you tell a child to write an essay as homework; they are bound to download the content to present before you the next day, baffling you by the interest of the many others lying in the queue. The parents often think of this as a menace from the challenging work wisdom they possess to earn their daily living. Their frames are not yet over with more demands for the CD-Burner and Scanner for more computing and smart-study, as they call it. The only option available to the poor parents of the IT age is to ponder for solace and to accept novel ways to convince their future generations regarding motivations and guided involvement.

The march from Web 1.0 to 2.0 and now to 3.0 offers every today's student the requisite to be IT enabled by chalk and the cheese. The TEACHERS need to further harness the requirements to the best of their abilities and interest. They need to depend on some SMART teaching options available in the classroom to make the learning scenario enjoyable for the kids. E-learning viz. DESTINATION SUCCESS is one such solution for Teachers. This offers an innovative methodology to educate every country's child with specialisation in the art of scalability involving people, processes and technology—the focus applies towards periodically building innovative capabilities and performance at the institutional level. The scenario today examines the requirement of a classroom equipped with an LCD projector and facility for computer-mediated instructions of the type that will aid the teacher in developing a quality teaching-learning environment. Specifically, such a classroom must have:

a.

A projection or display device can project a sufficiently large image to be viewed by every student in the classroom without causing eyestrain.

b.

An electronic interactive whiteboard system

c.

Computer with UPS System

d.

Education content library mapped to CBSE curriculum/ State Board Curriculum covering all significant subjects across all grades.

e.

Electronic Response system for each student to enable real-time assessment.

f.

Resource person to help teachers on a day-to-day basis to use the digital classroom systems.

About The Author

Dheeraj Mehrotra, MS, MPhil, PhD (Education Management) honoris causa., a white and a yellow belt in SIX SIGMA, a Certified NLP Business Diploma holder, is an Educational Innovator, Author, with expertise in Six Sigma In Education, Academic Audits, Neuro-Linguistic Programming (NLP), Total Quality Management In Education, an Experiential Educator, a CBSE Resource towards School Assessment (SQAA), CCE, JIT, Five S, and KAIZEN. He has authored over 100 books on topics which include Computer Science, AI, Digital Body Language, NLP, Quality Circles,

School Management, Classroom Effectiveness and Safety and security in schools. A former Principal at De Indian Public School, New Delhi, (INDIA), NPS International School, Guwahati, and Education Officer at GEMS, Gurgaon, with an ample teaching experience of over Two Decades, he is a certified Trainer for Quality Circles/ TQM in Education and QCI Standards for School Accreditation/ School Audits and Management. He has also been honoured with the President of India's National Teacher Award in the year 2006 and the Best Science Teacher State Award (By the Ministry of Science and Technology, State of UP), Innovation in Education for his inception of Six Sigma In Education by Education Watch, New Delhi and Education World- Best Teacher Award, BOLT Learner Teacher Award by Air India, 'Innovation in Education Award 2016' by Higher Education Forum (HEF), Gujarat Chapter, among others. He has developed over 150 FREE EDUCATIONAL MOBILE Apps for the Google Play Store exclusively for Teachers, Students, and Parents. This work has been recognised by the LIMCA BOOK OF RECORDS & INDIA BOOK OF RECORDS as the only Indian to draw that feast. Dr Mehrotra works as a PRINCIPAL at KUNWARS GLOBAL SCHOOL, Lucknow, in India. He has conducted over 1000 workshops globally on "Excellence In Education" integrated with Total Quality Management and Six Sigma, Technology Integration in Education (TIE), Developing towards being ROCKSTAR TEACHERS, including Cyberspace, Cyber Security, Classroom Management, School Leadership & Management, and Innovative teaching within classrooms via Mind Maps, NLP and Experiential Learning in Academics. He is an active TEDx speaker and can be viewed on the youtube TEDx channel.

As a premium UDEMY Instructor, he has developed over 450 courses and caters to over 8 Lakh students from 180 countries.

He can be visited at www.authordheerajmehrotra.com

BY NATIONAL
AWARDEE
EDUCATOR
Digital List Price: ₹ 72.45
M.R.P.: ₹ 199.00
Kindle Price: ₹ 69.00
Save ₹ 130.00 (65%)
inclusive of all taxes
101
SCHOOL
MANAGEMENT
STRATEGIES
Towards EFFECTIVE
QUALITY MANAGEMENT
System in Schools
DR. DHEERAJ
MEHROTRA
authordheerajmehrotra.com
Flipkart
available at
amazon

www.ingramcontent.com/pod-product-compliance
Lightning Source LLC
Chambersburg PA
CBHW030810170726
47995CB00011B/413